The
CHRISTMAS
SKY

The Christmas Sky

By FRANKLYN M. BRANLEY

Illustrated by Blair Lent

THOMAS Y. CROWELL COMPANY, NEW YORK

Also by the Author

A BOOK OF SATELLITES FOR YOU

A BOOK OF PLANETS FOR YOU

A BOOK OF ASTRONAUTS FOR YOU

A BOOK OF MOON ROCKETS FOR YOU

A BOOK OF THE MILKY WAY GALAXY FOR YOU

Published in Canada by Fitzhenry & Whiteside Limited, Toronto
Library of Congress Catalog Card No. AC 66-10053

ISBN 0-690-19342-4, 0-690-19343-2 (LB)

4   5   6   7   8   9   10

The CHRISTMAS SKY

The Bible tells us that many centuries ago in Judaea, a child was born of Mary, the wife of Joseph. The child was called Jesus.

The birth of every child is an important event in the life of his parents, his aunts and uncles, and other members of his family. But this birth was especially important. According to the Bible, the event caused great excitement. Men came from far away to see the child and bring Him gifts.

Many people, when they heard of the birth, were joyful. They hoped that Jesus would show the world the road to peace and brotherhood.

But some of the rulers of that time feared that Jesus would become more powerful than they themselves were. In many different ways they tried to destroy Jesus and the men and women who believed in Him. Finally Jesus was sentenced to die. Jesus died while He was still a young man, but the lessons He taught during His short life are studied today by people everywhere.

The coming of Jesus, or the Christ child, marked the beginning of Christianity. Since His time the teachings of Jesus have spread around the world. Millions of men have found happiness by learning His lessons and by living in the way He directed.

We know only one story of the birth of Jesus, the one that is told in the Bible. If other stories were written, they do not exist today. For centuries historians, scholars, and priests have tried to find more about the birth of Jesus, the first Christmas, an event so important that it changed the history of the world.

One of the things the Bible tells us is that a star appeared in the heavens at the time of Jesus' birth. The Gospel according to St. Matthew, chapter II, verses 1 and 2, says:

> Now when Jesus was born in Bethlehem of Judaea in the days of Herod the King, behold, there came wise men from the east to Jerusalem,
> Saying, Where is he that is born King of the Jews? for we have seen his star in the east, and are come to worship him.

Astronomers have wondered what this star might have been. They, too, are interested in learning the whole story of Jesus' birth. They have searched through records to discover what the sky was like when Jesus was born.

The star that the Wise Men saw must have been an unusual one, for it is not in the sky today. Except for certain "new" stars that astronomers can explain, the stars we see today are the same ones that men knew two thousand years ago. But there is no star which can be identified as the bright star that the Wise Men saw, the one they followed to find the manger in Bethlehem.

What, then, could this star have been to which the Bible refers? And where is it now?

Perhaps the "star" was not a star at all.

The streaks of light we see in the sky and call shooting stars are really not stars. They are meteors. They are made when small bits of material, sometimes as light and feathery as ashes, enter our atmosphere and become very hot. People of long ago could not tell comets and meteors from stars. They thought meteors were stars falling out of the sky.

Could the star of the Wise Men, the Star of Bethlehem, have been a "shooting star"? Could it have been an especially brilliant meteor that streaked across the sky?

This does not seem likely. Meteors are not rare. Even brilliant ones are seen occasionally. The Magi would not have been impressed by a meteor. The "star" the Wise Men saw must have been in the sky for weeks and months, all through the time that they journeyed to Bethlehem. If so, the object could not have been a meteor, for meteors last only seconds. They come and go so fast that sometimes you aren't even sure you have seen one.

Long ago, as today, comets appeared from time to time. Comets are wispy, cloudlike formations of gases and cosmic dust that reflect sunlight. They are members of the solar system. Like planets, they are held in orbit by the attraction of the sun. Frequently comets appear that are large enough and bright enough to be seen clearly without a telescope. They may be visible for several days, weeks, or sometimes for months.

Because people did not understand comets in those days, they used to call them "long-haired stars." The gaseous comet tails reminded them of long, streaming hair.

Could it have been a comet that appeared in the sky around the time of the birth of Jesus? A comet might have remained in the sky for days, weeks, or even for months. If it had been bright, it would have attracted the attention of everyone. People would have seen it and wondered if the comet was a sign of some special event.

Astronomers of today understand comets and the paths that they follow. They can figure the paths so accurately that they know which comets were close enough to the earth to be seen hundreds and even thousands of years ago. And they know that there was no bright comet visible around the time of Jesus' birth. If there had been a comet, people would not have been happy to see it. They would have been afraid. A comet was thought to be the finger of a god pointing toward the earth, warning everyone to beware of danger and calamity. Comets were looked upon as signs of disaster; they were "evil stars" associated with famines and floods, earthquakes and disease, and never with happy events. So it seems unlikely that the Star of Bethlehem could have been a comet.

In 1604, a German astronomer named Johann Kepler one night saw a star appear where before there had been no star. The star grew brighter and brighter each passing day. It grew so bright that it could be seen in the daytime. Then the star faded and rapidly disappeared.

Such a star is called a nova, from the Latin word for new. Kepler suggested that the Star of Bethlehem may have been a nova. Surely such a bright, new object would have impressed all who saw it. And such a star would have been seen for several weeks and so could have served as a guide for the Wise Men. But astronomers know that, although new stars have appeared on many occasions down through history, there was no new star in the sky anywhere near the time that we believe Jesus was born.

There were, however, "wandering stars" in the sky around the time Jesus was born. "Wandering stars" are what we today call "planets." If so, one of these could have been the sign that told the Wise Men a king had been born.

Because we know how long it takes planets to go around the sun, astronomers can figure out the position of each planet in the sky at any time in history. If it is possible to determine when Jesus was born, we can find out which planets could be seen at that time. It is customary to assume that Jesus was born in the year 1. But there is good evidence that He must have been born some time before that.

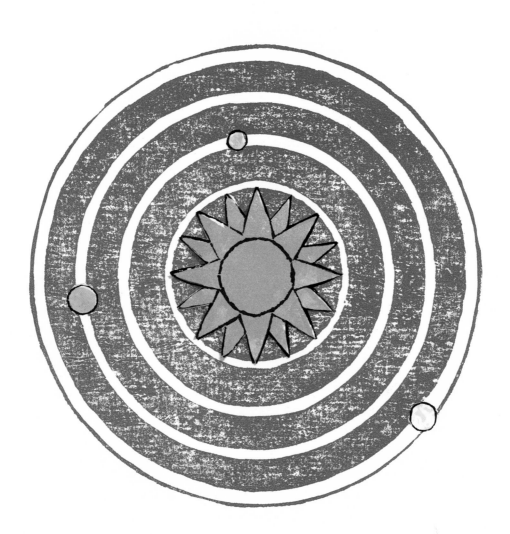

Around A.D. 93, a man called Flavius Josephus wrote a history of the Jewish people. In one part of his history he described the events that occurred at the time of Jesus' birth: "Now it happened that during the high priesthood of Matthias, there was another person made high priest for a single day, that very day which the Jews observe as a feast, and that very night there was an eclipse of the moon."

Josephus went on to say that the new high priest was appointed because of the sickness of King Herod, a brief sickness from which the king shortly died. Herod was king of Jerusalem at the time of Jesus' birth. The feast to which Josephus refers was probably Purim, a Jewish religious observance. Because we know the feast was held at the time when an eclipse occurred, the passage above provides clues to the time of Herod's death. Astronomers know there was a partial eclipse of the moon on March 13 in the year now referred to as 4 B.C. It was the only eclipse that occurred on or near any religious festival day for several years on either side of 4 B.C.

Therefore Herod must have died a short time after March 13 in 4 B.C. So Jesus must have been born in 4 B.C., or sometime earlier.

We turn from the writings of Josephus to the Bible to find out just how much earlier the event might have happened.

Herod had heard of the birth of Jesus. He commanded the Wise Men who were going to the birthplace of Jesus to be brought before him in Jerusalem, and asked them to return to him after they had found the child and tell him exactly where the child was. Then Herod himself could go to honor Him.

But the Wise Men did not return to Jerusalem. The Bible tells us that angels came to the Wise Men, warning them that Herod did not really want to worship Jesus; rather, he planned to destroy Him. So the Wise Men returned to their own country by another route.

Herod was angry at their disobedience. Because of his anger, and because he feared this infant child, Herod ordered a brutal murder. We read about it in the Gospel according to St. Matthew, chapter II, verse 16:

> Then Herod, when he saw that he was mocked of the wise men, was exceeding wroth, and sent forth, and slew all the children that were in Bethlehem, and in all the coasts thereof, from two years old and under, according to the time which he had diligently enquired of the wise men.

We do not know exactly how long it was from the time when Herod saw the Wise Men until the time when they were to return to Jerusalem to report to him. It must have been no longer than two years, for Herod, in order to be sure that Jesus was destroyed, gave an order that all children two years old, or younger, should be slain.

The Bible gives us another clue that leads us to believe Jesus was born some time before A.D. 1. In chapter II, verses 1-7, of the Gospel according to St. Luke we read:

> And it came to pass in those days, that there went out a decree from Caesar Augustus, that all the world should be taxed.
>
> And all went to be taxed, every one into his own city.
> And Joseph also went up from Galilee, out of the city of Nazareth, into Judaea, unto the city of David, which is called Bethlehem, (because he was of the house and lineage of David,)
>
> To be taxed with Mary his espoused wife, being great with child.
>
> And so it was, that, while they were there, the days were accomplished that she should be delivered.
>
> And she brought forth her firstborn son, and wrapped him in swaddling clothes, and laid him in a manger; because there was no room for them in the inn.

Two thousand years ago the Roman Empire spread all around the Mediterranean Sea, and every person in the empire had to pay whatever taxes the emperor demanded. During the reign of Caesar Augustus, Emperor of the Romans, three tax orders were sent out to the people. We know this from the inscription on a stone tablet uncovered by archaeologists working near Ankara, Turkey, in 1923. This tablet, an inscription from a Roman temple, was a record of many events of the times, and it included the three great tax orders. One of these orders was issued in the year we now call 8 B.C.

Many scholars think this order included the entire Roman Empire. For the tax to be levied, each person had to return to the place where he was born so he could be counted and the tax could be collected. This is why so many people, Joseph and Mary among them, crowded into Judaea and into the small town of Bethlehem, known as the city of David.

You may wonder how this tax order, issued in 8 B.C., strengthens the belief that Jesus was born at least two years later. In the days of Caesar Augustus there was no quick way of letting people know of the orders made by their rulers, so tax collections were not made everywhere at the same time. Collectors journeyed from village to village, counting the people, charging the taxes, and collecting the money. They took weeks, months, even years to reach the outer boundaries of the empire. People returning to the place where they were born traveled overland by foot, or by donkey if they were fortunate. The journey was tedious and long; many months might pass between the time people first heard of the order and their arrival at the city of their birth. It was the tax order of 8 B.C. that caused Mary to be in Bethlehem when her days were accomplished and when Jesus was born.

Events around the time of Herod's death and records of the tax orders of Caesar Augustus lead to the same conclusion. Jesus was born sometime between 8 B.C. and 4 B.C., probably in the year 6 B.C.

We can also find out the season of the year when He was born.

Long ago a few Christians celebrated the birth of Jesus in December as we do today. There were good reasons why these Christians held their celebrations in the month of December. In the early days of Christianity, those who were Christians dared not reveal their identity to the Romans, for it was a crime to be a Christian. Christians were put in chains, or they were forced to participate in barbarous Roman games where they were attacked by wild animals.

Since they could not reveal their identity, Christians had to find secret places and secret ways to celebrate the birth of Jesus. Small groups would meet together in the dark, cold catacombs, which were burial places deep below the streets of Rome. Other groups celebrated Christmas on a Roman festival day that came during the Saturnalia, a period of gaiety in those days. The Saturnalia was a happy time: gifts were exchanged, people danced in the streets, and decorated their homes with flowers and boughs. The climax of the Saturnalia occurred December 25.

Because all Rome was joyful on this day, the Christians would not stand out from the crowd. They could celebrate the birth of Jesus freely. The Romans would think they were happy because of the Saturnalia.

December 25 had been an important day for centuries, since the ancient times when men worshipped the sun. The sun was an important god then, a god essential to life itself.

In summer, the sun was high above the horizon, and bathed the countryside with warmth. Crops flourished and there was an abundance of food. As fall and winter approached, the position of the noonday sun became lower and lower. The countryside was bleak and cold. Plants died in the field. There was always great alarm at this time; suppose the sun continued its movement toward the horizon. Suppose it moved lower, and lower, and lower—finally to disappear completely and never to return again. Without the sun, life could not go on. For several days celebrations were held to keep the sun god from leaving the sky. The first day of winter was the time of greatest joy, for after that the sun was a bit higher with each passing day.

According to our present calendar, the first day of winter occurs on December 21 or 22. But there have been many different kinds of calendars down through the centuries. In one of these winter began on December 25 rather than December 22. It was by this calendar that the Saturnalia was celebrated. The noise and excitement of these celebrations, intended for a quite different purpose, obscured the joy of the Christians who were celebrating the birth of Jesus.

In the early part of the fourth century, persecution of the Christians ended. At that time, the Emperor Constantine, who was himself a Christian, decreed that the birth of Jesus should be celebrated on December 25. This date has since then become the day of celebration of the Nativity in many parts of the world.

However, Jesus' birth most likely occurred in the springtime. Once more the Bible gives the important clue. In Chapter II, verse 8, of the Gospel according to St. Luke we read:

> And there were in the same country shepherds abiding in the field, keeping watch over their flock by night.

In Judaea, today as long ago, the month of December is cold and rainy. It is the time when flocks are taken into corrals, sheltered from wind and rain. In the springtime, after the weather has moderated, the sheep are taken into the fields. Only in the springtime do shepherds keep watch over their flocks through the night, for spring is the season when lambs are born and the lambs must be protected.

So it seems reasonable to believe that Jesus was born in the springtime, probably in the year 6 B.C. Astronomers can determine many of the events that occurred in the sky at that time. They know what planets were above the horizon, the positions they occupied, and the manner in which they moved.

The tables of the motions and positions of planets as recorded by astronomers show that there were three planets in the evening skies of the fall and winter of 7 B.C., continuing into the spring of 6 B.C., and that these planets moved closer together as the months went by.

The three planets were Mars, Jupiter, and Saturn. Saturn was in the constellation of Pisces, the fishes. Jupiter was a bit below and to the north. Mars was much lower and toward the south.

As the weeks and months of the fall and winter of 7 B.C. and the early months of 6 B.C. passed by, the planets moved closer and closer together. In the late winter and early spring the planets formed a small triangle in the constellation Pisces.

Most people did not see this triangle. The planets were low in the western sky and they set beneath the horizon before the sky had become deeply dark.

But the Magi knew about the planets. They were astrologers. Being astrologers, they studied the planets; they knew of their positions and their motions. They knew that the three planets were in a constellation where centuries earlier, according to Jewish rabbis, planets had appeared three years previous to the birth of Moses. He was the prophet who was to return the Israelites out of Egypt to the eastern borders of the promised land. Pisces was therefore considered the national constellation of the Jews, as well as a tribal symbol.

This may have been a sign to the Magi that an event of great importance was occurring in the land of the Jews. The Star of Christmas might have been these three planets, close together in Pisces. They may have been the guide that the Wise Men followed to find the manger where Jesus was born.

Perhaps so. However, there are many people who believe that the Star of Bethlehem was not a group of planets, nor an exploding star, nor an especially brilliant meteor or comet. These people believe that the star was like nothing men had ever seen before, and that its appearance will never be understood by men. They believe that it was a miracle star.

Possibly we will never know what the Star of Christmas really was. But no matter what it may have been, the sign that appeared in the sky that first Christmas will always have deep meaning to millions of people. For the coming of Jesus brought a promise of peace on earth and good will to men.

About the Author

Franklyn M. Branley, Chairman, Astronomer, and former Director of Educational Services at the American Museum-Hayden Planetarium, is the author of many books about astronomy and other sciences for young people. He holds degrees from New York University, Columbia University, and the State University of New York College at New Paltz.

The Christmas Sky is based on the very popular lectures which Dr. Branley and other members of the staff have given to hundreds of thousands of people at the Hayden Planetarium during each Christmas season.

Dr. Branley and his wife live in Woodcliff Lake, New Jersey.

About the Illustrator

Blair Lent has written, as well as illustrated, several books for children. One of the books he has illustrated, *The Wave*, was chosen as a runner-up for the 1965 Caldecott Medal and was named one of the ten best illustrated children's books of 1964 by *The New York Times*. His work has also appeared in the AIGA Fifty Best Books of the Year Show and in The AIGA Children's Book Show.

Mr. Lent was born in Boston and was graduated with honors from the Boston Museum School. As a recipient of a Cummings Traveling Scholarship, he studied in Europe for one year. Mr. Lent lives in Cambridge, Massachusetts.